D0875954

FROG CROAKS

FROG CROAKS

Haiku Tongue in Cheek

by Carl Oldenburg

Illustrated by Jonathan M. Nelson

CROWN PUBLISHERS, INC.
NEW YORK

© 1975 by Carl Oldenburg
Illustrations © 1975 by Jonathan M. Nelson

Printed in the United States of America
Published simultaneously in Canada by General Publishing
Company Limited

Library of Congress Cataloging in Publication Data

Oldenburg, Carl.
  Frog croaks.

    1.   Haiku—Anecdotes, facetiae, satire, etc.
I.   Title.
PN6231.H2804   895.6'1'07   75-19095
ISBN 0-517-52341-8

With Apologies To The Entire Japanese Nation

INTRODUCTION

Japanese haiku is a poetic form consisting of a three-line, nonrhyming verse of 17 syllables presented in a 5–7–5 scheme. Unlike much of Western poetry, the appreciation of which depends upon the understanding of complex symbolism, the haiku poem means no more than it says and can, therefore, be enjoyed by all.

Though most of the subjects of haiku are found in nature, there is no subject to which haiku may not be addressed. However, the verses may not be intellectual, nor may they be emotional. They present a picture, or an image, and whether or not the reader is given to think or to feel will depend upon relationships presented in the picture.

For the reader already familiar with this poetic form, the rewards will be as great as for the uninitiated. Years of painstaking research have resulted in the presentation, here, of verses found translated *nowhere else* in the English-speaking world. Further, and almost unbelievably, this book presents a host of poets heretofore unknown to the Western reader. It is as though the Japanese had contrived to keep the best of their beloved haiku from Western eyes. My discoveries, I would add, give me tremendous pride and satisfaction, not because of the many jealousies they will certainly arouse among my literary colleagues but because I have succeeded in making these treasures available to all. But we will not learn the haiku way by talking about it. We shall hasten, now, to the verses themselves. And so, dear reader, fasten your safety belts, for we are off to the land of the setting sun.

THE VERSES

Greeted by smiles
All day long and life is sweet
Drat! My fly's open.

(KINKI)

This verse of Kinki's is instructive to other poets. It is a warning against the major enemy of any promising artist—public acceptance. The poet must set himself apart from popular social currents and practice humility. In this way, he gains the solitude and selflessness required for truly creative effort. Among Occidentals, the natural body odor of the poet serves to accomplish this purpose.

Absolute silence
Except for the sound of the birds
Breaking the wind.

(BASSO)

The old Basso is sitting outside on a lovely evening late in the Spring of the year. All is still save for the fishing birds which dart by at the edge of the water. As is obvious, Basso had developed the art of directing his senses to nature to a remarkable degree. Few since his time have achieved this measure of receptivity. A doubting student of Basso's once challenged the old master saying:

"Master, I think you are hearing things." To which the old Basso replied:

"And what else would one hear, small toad?"

> *What tiny stranger*
> *Rests upon the Autumn leaf?*
> *Oh! Butterfly poop.*

(BASSO)

Basso was not only a peerless master of hai-ku, he was also an effective and tireless teacher of the form. As we have explained, nature's living creations are the major topics of haiku and, as might be expected, many eager young students take to the woodlands with a vengeance. The old master wrote this verse to reveal the difference between a sober contemplation of nature on the one hand, and being a bit too damned nosey on the other.

Cherry blossoms bloom
On the branches in my yard
The horny season.

(BASSO)

Here the old Basso is commenting on his age if not actually lamenting over it. The whole point of the verse is that Basso's "inner reminder" of the season has failed him. The cherry blossoms substitute for it.

This haiku is often misinterpreted. It is true that Basso's school of haiku accepted coeds for the first time the very year he wrote these lines. However, the virgin coeds are not the cherry blossoms, nor the yard his school. It might further be noted that although a school of Hanki Panki did exist in the vicinity, there was no record of an exchange program.

> *My new house woman*
> *Skillfully cooks rice and peas*
> *In the same kettle.*

> (BASSO)

The old Basso presented this verse to his class and asked if anyone would care to make comments on it. Nearly all of the students, thinking it to be one of the Master's own, said that they felt it was a fine haiku. But one student remained silent.

"Will you not give an opinion?" asked the Master. The young man reddened and was timid, but finally he said:

"I am sorry, Master, but I would not even call it haiku. To me it sounds like some throwaway line out of a very bad Chinese joke book."

"Precisely," said the Master. "Now you and I shall talk of better things while your long-eared classmates continue to admire it."

And in this manner did the Old Basso keep his classes of manageable size.

Stopping in midstream
The riderless horse pauses
Splash! splash! splash! splash! splash!

(NOSHŌ)

One of the first of the old masters of haiku has instructed us that a verse which presents 70 to 80 percent of the physical image is a good verse, but that we shall never tire of a verse which presents only 50 to 60 percent. This haiku, written by Noshō, is an excellent case in point. The horse has come to a total halt. What then is causing the splashing noises? Are there some fish struggling through the shallows? Is there a waterfall nearby? Perhaps playful children are throwing stones into the water. Here we have unity, yet questions remain. This is the essence of true haiku.

The baker woman
Bends over her daily work
Ah! she's got nice buns.

(SNIKI)

Rich foods and exotic dishes have never been the fare of true haiku poets. In this verse, Sniki pays tribute to the simple basics of his existence.

The spring waterfall
Gushes forth its loud clatter
My bladder answers.

(ITSI BITSU)

Few haiku capture the Zen spirit of man's oneness with nature as does this verse. We can see Itsi Bitsu, caught up in the lively enthusiasm of the rushing water, dancing first on one foot, then on the other, tears of joy streaming down his face and lower limbs.

The quiet young child
Talks to the woodland creatures
He has a screw loose.

(SPIFFI)

The haiku poet has his feet on the ground
and lays no claim to extraordinary or mystical
insight. He sees what is there and no more. This is
the point of the old poet's verse. Feeling a sym-
pathy toward the boy, old Spiffi gave him a brilliant but fake gem stone, round cut, and of approximately four carats, and he said to him:

"If, as the years pass, the muddy waters in
your poor head do not clear, then learn English
and place this worthless stone in your navel. You
will find that many Westerners will pay you
handsomely for whatever nonsense falls from
your lips. Wearing a cheap nightgown will help.
And do not fear—Buddha will forgive you."
Today, that boy (now middle-aged) makes more
money than Billy Graham.

What a mystery!
I walk through green pastures, yet
Brown stains on my feet.

(KINKI)

The green pastures, of course, are life itself. It is most interesting that Kinki wrote this verse in his later years and not in his youth as the reader would have guessed. To see an inherent mystery in all things is characteristic of the extremely insightful and of the extremely dumb. It must have been a source of pain to Kinki that popular consensus in his own time was not flattering to him.

> *That look in her eye*
> *One day many years ago—*
> *Jeez, I missed my chance!*

> (KINKI)

As the reader may infer from this verse, Kinki was possessed of a rather slow mental velocity. This characteristic of the poet has been brought out rather humorously by several of the critics of haiku. If one looks at some of the requirements of this form, Kinki's "problem" will become clear.

The haiku is, conventionally, 17 syllables in length. Interestingly, this is approximately the number of syllables which the average individual utters in one breath. And, it is about as long in time as the haiku experience itself, or the duration of the "haiku moment." The mind, suddenly, perceives the image or gains the insight. And the mind, seeing the image, says, "Ahh!" (or "Ooops," or "Wow!" or "Yeech!"—depending on exactly what is perceived—but, generically, "Ahh!") Seeing the "Ah-ness" of things took Kinki much longer than most; hence, his critics talk not of his "haiku moment" but of a "haiku half-hour."

These same sorts of remarks were made of Kinki while he lived and they did not bother him one whit. In fact, on one occasion he is said to have remarked, "Please to tell whatsa rush? The old masters themselves only grind out about ten good three-liners in their whole miserable existence."

These winter showers
Nostrils so stuffed I can't tell
Which son has come home.

(BLASTU)

The account of the old poet Blastu and his two sons almost takes on the proportions of a fable. One son was as good as the other one was bad. The good boy was continually lighting joss sticks to please Buddha, but, in so doing, he filled his father's house with the stifling aromas of cheap incense. The other son, out of sheer meanness some thought, was a chronic windbreaker. On nights when both boys were home, the unhappy poet, unable to stand conditions inside the house, would sleep out-of-doors.

Shortly after this verse was written, a small miracle occurred for Blastu. The good son happened to be standing too close to his brother as he struck a match to light one of his joss sticks. Though the gas explosion was minor, it cured the good son of lighting and the other son of letting. Though Blastu did not exactly live happily ever after (the boys remained at home), he was at least able to breathe in his own house.

The cold autumn wind
Swirling up her homely skirts
The old matron scowls.

(NITO)

Portending winter, the icy wind from the Sea of Okhotsk swirls around gnarled limbs and into dark crevices. We see an old woman of Nito's village muttering vainly against the stiff gusts which drown out her cryptic utterances.

Nito's old master was pleased with this verse and complimented him on the imagery of this late-autumn haiku.

"I shiver just to read it," he said to his young student. Nito, noticing the discomfort and sadness in his old mentor's eyes, quoted optimistically from the Western poet Shelley:

"If Winter comes, can Spring be far behind?"

The wiser of the two then replied in a soft but resolute voice:

"You bet your kakusaza it can!"

My neighbor's young son
Has got himself a girl friend
But doesn't know why.

(BLESSU)

This verse does not translate easily and has been greatly misunderstood. The last line of the poem is sometimes translated:

But doesn't know it.

And sometimes as

But doesn't know how.

Such alternate translations, of course, render entirely different literal meanings to the verse. But all the concern (a heated argument has raged for three and a half centuries) is actually irrelevant. The last line is not a pivotal one; it is a mere afterthought, or a concession to the 5–7–5 form. If one *ignores* the third line, one has the poem! When the reader stops at the end of the second line, he realizes the verse is complete and his mind immediately recalls the words of Heinrich Kley, who said precisely the same thing in his charming German prose:

"Wenn zwei vor Gott sich einig sind und ihre Zahnbürsten bei sich haben, gehort ihnen die ganze Welt." °

° For the unschooled, we translate: "When a little boy and girl are with God, and have their little toothbrushes along—the whole world is theirs!"

How simple after all! Incidentally, it was this interpretation, this solution, if you will, of one of Japan's most puzzling haiku which won this author the coveted Ahshiti Award in 1961.

> *Full of the new wine,*
> *Father comes rattling home*
> *Through the bamboo stalks.* °

(KINKI)

This is a very successful Spring verse. The moon is full, and by it the poet sees Blotso, his father, coming home. The warm winds of the new season rustle the sprightly bamboo, though to Kinki it is as though his father is making all the sounds of the night. The haiku is as warm and vibrant as the gentle arrival of the Spring breezes themselves. Blotso's wife (the poet's mother), when presented with the verse some days later, failed to grasp the image. She grasped Blotso, as did he, later, his son, the poet.

° The attentive reader may notice that in translating into English, we have sometimes failed in the 5–7–5 count requirement. It does not happen often, and for these tabulations we wish to acknowledge the efforts of Mr. Eugene Feathers, who learned the new math at Pensacola Junior College and who did a masterful and near-perfect job for us.

My love's too busy
To hear the song in my heart—
She's picking her nose.

(ITSI BITSU)

This well-known verse has given millions of Japanese cause for mirth ever since Professor LeRoy Burnstedder translated it in 1962. The last line actually reads (in the original):

She's *pinching* her nose.

The Japanese have flat noses and there is a widespread folk belief, taken half seriously, that repeated nose-pinching will make the nose more prominent, thus producing a profile more like that of the Japanese aristocracy. Burnstedder, as now everyone knows, has the poor girl *picking* her nose and he never lived the mistake down.

He claimed that a typographical error had been made, but his colleagues wouldn't allow it. They all greeted him with what came to be called the "Burnstedder Salute" (which simply amounted to thrusting one's finger into a nostril and grinning devilishly). Professor Burnstedder has not been seen in public since 1967.

Schizophrenia
And I thought I was really sick
I am beside myself.

(KINKI)

Not true haiku, of course, this pitiful verse is included that a lesson might be learned. As a young pupil, Kinki was merely venturing into the realm of wit. No student of haiku can afford schizophrenia. Blessed are the poor for their ailments shall be limited to prickly heat, stomachache, and common diarrhea (to remind the reader of old Basso's wisdom on this point). His fellow students showed no appreciation of this departure from the way of haiku. One classmate quickly penned the following verse and attached it to the back of Kinki's blouse:

Posing as a nut
Melon's gay colors reveal
He's just a big fruit.

This missile, which Kinki did not discover until the hour of his bath the following month, pained him to the quick (hitting home as it did). The employment of wit invites destruction.

My neighbor's quick step
Is it that his son returns
Or diarrhea?

(BASSO)

Many feel that this haiku represents Basso's worst, or perhaps, only failure. Most critics see the old poet spending his remaining days on a bankrupted chicken farm near Kumamota, his world shrunken down to such irrelevant matters as that addressed in this verse, and his senile mind reduced to the delusion that such questions are important.

A more astute minority, however, agrees that this verse is actually among the old Basso's best efforts. It is not the substance of the question that matters; it is that mankind *questions,* and that a man's life is but a succession of questions. Basso's question, as posed in this verse, was never satisfactorily answered. The neighbor suddenly slowed his pace; his gait became awkward; his shoulders sagged; and his face showed signs of genuine despair. He shuffled out of sight and never, on subsequent meetings with Basso, spoke of the incident.

Uncle arrested.
For fondling a mannequin
Our shades drawn tonight.

(ONNŌ)

Haiku must not proclaim emotion. If emotion is to be conveyed, it must come through in the image presented. This poem by Onnō is an excellent example on this point. The embarrassment to Onnō and his family must have been overwhelming in the shame-based culture of Japan. To make matters even worse, it was just a week before that the reputation of the family had

already been tainted by the rumor that Onnō's eleven-year-old sister was the "phantom poet" of the local railway station.

Frost on the gallows
As the condemned one is hanged
A nip in the air.

(SONASTI)

When Omagoshi's School of Haiku was to graduate its first class of students, the head of the school had decided to honor the leading pupil by allowing him to present a valedictory address to an assembly of parents, faculty, community leaders, and visiting poets. The student was also to present one verse, kept from the world until the close of his address.

The youthful poet, Sonasti, the best of his class, rendered this haiku. So compelling was the imagery of a cold, remorseless death that the verse put a chill over the entire gathering. It left the head of the school particularly cold.

Do my eyes play tricks?
Does the rice move in the bowl?
Oh ish! it's maggots.

(YUKKI)

Judged by many critics to be the perfect haiku in every requirement, Yukki's verse, for some inexplicable reason, did not become popular with the people of Japan. Popular taste is, ultimately, impossible to explain.

My sister's brassiere—
Right in my own house we have
Pockets of poverty.

(SPIFFI)

Normally, the true haiku poet abstains from employing the form in social commentary. Spiffi, however, was apparently unable to resist. He clearly saw that Japanese industrialism was bringing Westernization with it. Not only had Japan begun to adopt Western modes of dress but also the Western (negative) attitude toward the blessed state of poverty. He became an avid traditionalist and at the close of his famous speech to the House of Councilors his emotions overcame him and he shouted the now famous slogan, "Down with the blouse! Up with the kimono!"

> *Go away fat toad!*
>   *My wife's mother is coming*
>   *To do your duties.*

(BLASTU)

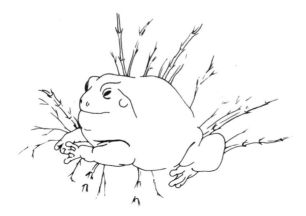

This haiku is often misunderstood by the Western reader who is apt to assume that it is derogatory and insulting. This is most definitely not the case. Those not familiar with Japanese folk beliefs may naïvely suppose that a toad's only "duty" consists of sitting about looking ugly. In fact, however, the toad is perceived as embodying a protective spirit, and each member of a household which has its toad is kept from all harm.

It is true, but only coincidentally, that Blastu's mother-in-law had developed the knack of catching flying insects with a quick flick of her active tongue.

That lithe girl next door
Out each night with amateurs
It pains my poor heart.

(BASSO)

It was always difficult for the old Basso to imagine that anyone might prefer the verses of the younger poets to his own; even if the listener were not a particularly discriminating one. Indeed, it must have pained him to see his young students enjoying their eager audiences.

We might note here that Professor Bings-

wyler insisted on a sexual frustration theme when
he translated this verse in 1913. In that interpretation, however, he revealed Bingswyler's
character and not Basso's. Careful examination
of the old Basso's biography makes it abundantly
clear that, with one small exception, the old
master did not have a lecherous bone in his body.

> *Our wedding night*
> *Lotus Blossom views her prize*
> *And is not smiling.*

> (ITSI BITSU)

A wedding verse by Itsi Bitsu reveals his
approval of his bride. She is, we would have to
imagine, inwardly excited by the gift (bride's
prize) which she has just discovered, but she
controls her joy in deference to the solemnity of
the moment.

The following two verses by Noshō are presented as haiku which fail because they are sen-
timental. In both cases, the haiku experience is
contaminated by doting paternalism:

> *My love for my son*
> *Not lessened because of the*
> *BB in my leg.*

And,

> *Butterfly wings outspread*
> *Upon the cool dry rock where*
> *Hubert tore them off.*

For a father to reveal such immense pride in his son is not unusual, but such pride can never produce a haiku. Neither could the loss of a son produce a haiku; nor the winning of the national lottery; nor a brilliant idea. Now—a gnat caught in one's ear! *That* can produce real haiku.

Hubert is, of course, an odd name for a Japanese parent to give to his son. It has been popular in Japan in modern times, however, because of the tremendous popularity of a recent Vice President of the United States. The Japanese have great admiration for a man who can give a

profound oration at the drop of a hat, a leaf, a
snowflake, a particle of dandruff, or whatever.

> *The ape in the cage*
> *Beckons to his family*
> *And points at my son.*

(NOSHŌ)

Surprisingly, Noshō's last haiku on his son is
a fairly good one. The self-advertising of a proud
parent is absent in this verse. The haiku insight is
there. The zoo is there. But Noshō has not been
back.

> *Her mother's figure*
> *Ghastly prototype of the*
> *Shape of things to come.*

(OSOSO)

In this verse, the poet's "haiku moment"
centers on his glimpse into the future. This is
unusual, for haiku are very much geared to the
present, and to *real*, not imagined, images. But it
is genuine. Ironically, it was the girl's father (who
wanted his daughter married worse than anyone)
who alerted the young poet. On an occasion when
all were assembled, the old man affectionately
regarded his wife, saying:

"Ishi-usu ni kimono wo kiesta ȳo," which, translated, means: "[You look] like a millstone dressed in a kimono."

It was immediately after that exchange that Ososo determined not to marry. An *appreciation* of the maturation processes of nature is one thing—setting up house with them is quite another.

> *Hark! tiny firefly,*
>   *Can't you make a brighter light?*
>   *I have wet my foot!*

(YAHU)

Yahu formed his own school of haiku in the latter part of the Messi Period. He devoted six days of the week to his writing and painting and the seventh to either sake or rice wine. The above verse was written on one of those "seventh days" as the old master stood outside his house on a moonless night.

It subsequently became famous as the original "drunk verse," of which each poet must write at least one. The "drunk verse" has been ignored by every historian of haiku in the Western world. Whatever the reasons, the oversight is unfortunate. Ignoring this facet of the haiku poets' total experience prevents us from seeing them as whole men and from analyzing their poetry in its full expression.

Interestingly enough, many of the "drunk verses" were written in the snow, using what old Basso referred to as "man's first pen," and, understandably, these were soon lost to the world of literature. Those presented here were largely produced during dry winters and appeared on bar napkins and on TP parchment. Written at the height of a "glow" which, granted, is only the illusion of the "haiku moment," they nonetheless are expressions of the poet's art.

The following haiku is typical of many of the "drunk verses." It was written by Kinki for whom it came as a pure inspiration while the young poet was standing in the corner with a paper lantern over his head:

> *Ho! A butterfly!*
> *A pretty little butterfly.*
> *How about that, guys!*

The verse is said to have moved every member of his party to tears. The poet spent the greater part of the evening producing auto-graphed copies for everyone at hand. By the following morning, however, its literary merit had been sharply reassessed.

Among the better "drunk verses" to come out of the Messi Period are the following:

> *Laden with nectar*
> *The overripe wistaria*
> *Falls flat on its face.*

(OSOSO)

> *Deftly the town drunk*
> *Masters the rolling sidewalk*
> *What artist has more skill?*

(KINKI)

Two drunks in the alley
  Leaning against one another
  A pissing duet.

(KRUMMI)

Though the tradition of the "drunk verse" continues, few of the modern efforts match these of the Messi Period.

The November winds
Invade my fragile outhouse
Please nature, hurry!

(BASSO)

There is something very forced about this haiku. It does not have the sense of action and movement which one comes to expect from Basso's verses.

My dog's daily trips
To the tree I planted made
A lovely bonsai.

(OSOSO)

Here is the Horatio Alger story of impoverished poets, or better still, it is a tribute to the patience and wisdom of the true haiku poet. No doubt Ososo was many times tempted to discourage the dog who so severely stunted his tree, but he did not. Ultimately, he knew that this too was the way of nature. But his genius did intervene, for once Ososo realized that the dwarfed tree would never grow any larger, he began bottling the secret formula, made a fortune off the bonsai devotees, took an expensive apartment near the Tokyo Airport, and never wrote another verse. Thus was lost to the world of haiku one of its most promising young masters.

> *Stooping for a coin*
> *I step on my poor fingers,*
> *A dime's worth of pain.*

> (SKRUFTI)

Here Skrufti shares with us his lesson in poverty. Walking the roadways and gutters, head bent, looking for lost money, subtracts from the beauty and dignity of the noble state of impoverishment. As the great Sniki once said, "If you can't rip off at least a couple of thousand, why bother?"

> *Delicate flowers*
> *On the sweet-scented tissue—*
> *What a fate for you!*

> (YOHUDI)

This modern verse has come to be known as "Yohudi's Puzzle." Written in 1956, it immediately became one of the most popular of all Japanese haiku. It was assumed that the image presented is one of an array of chrysanthemums spreading fragile petals against the "sweet-scented tissue" of a dew-laden May morning. Their "fate" was taken to refer to the spoiling effects of the strong sunshine which the long summer days would bring.

However, when this interpretation was brought to Yohudi's attention, he would break into a giggling fit, slapping his knees until tears of delight rolled down his cheeks. Understandably, the poet's reaction has given at least some of his critics cause to call their interpretation into question. To this day and, perhaps, for all time to come, the exact nature of the image in the poet's eye remains a mystery.

A terrible dream—
Great Buddha squatting over
Our little village!

(BASSO)

This haiku voices a common fear among the people of Basso's village. It is not at all clear why the residents of Komode should have developed their collective paranoia.

A vase from Aunt Mae
Who says that it's an antique
I think it's a crock.

(BLESSU)

Blessu's delight in examining his gift is apparent in this verse. We can see him turning the vase over and over in his hands, pondering not only the vessel's origin, but also the question of how to repay the old lady.

Six paces behind
Walks my obedient wife.
I hear a snicker!

(ITSI BITSU)

Several of the haiku poets wrote poems on the early symptoms of the women's liberation

movement. We present Itsi Bitsu's as a singular
and typical example of such verses. The married
poets, understandably, saw the early signs of the
movement long before the rest of society. In
1935, for example, Hushi wrote his verse on the
hair he found in his sūpu. In 1929, Onnō had
written a haiku on the almost imperceptible
movement of his wife's eyebrows the day he came
home quite late from the public baths. And, even
before Onnō, of course, Tushi had written his
verse on the wrinkle produced by the careless
folding of his snuggies.

> *A wedding gift comes*
> *From my maternal uncle—*
> *Ancient owl droppings.*

> (BINKI)

As in Western culture, the owl, which, unlike most birds, has its eyes in the front of its head
(the more resembling those of man), is thought
to be a wise creature. The uncle of Binki was
dependent on the charity of his relatives and,
hence, he could not afford to give them the bird.
It is, after all, the thought that counts.

> *The first thing one needs*
> *In making a lovely dish*
> *Is to have hot woks.*

> (SNIKI)

A major theme in the Japanese pavilion at the Chicago World's Fair of 1933 was the introduction of oriental cooking to the outside world. Sniki was commissioned by the Imperial Minister of the Culinary Arts to compose this haiku for the frontispiece of a complimentary cookbook printed in English.

The officials who manned the pavilion booth were surprised that many of the ladies would blush upon opening the little book. When Japan's leading chef quoted this haiku aloud to one visitor, she felled him with a purse full of souvenir coins, thus causing an international incident.

I SHOWED HIM WHAT'S COOKING

read the headlines of a Chicago newspaper the following day in quoting the burly matron who had laid the poor man out.

> *A small yellow bird*
> *Drops his warm greeting*
> *On the boss's Lincoln.*

(OSOSO)

Ososo's verse reveals a difference between Western and Oriental viewpoints. The Western mind tends to see only competition and survival instincts operating between nature's species.

Here, in this verse, Ososo reveals the cordial side of nature. Too, the Western individual would doubtlessly insist:

"I would rather the bird had sung for me." But is not a song without substance?

> *I am not deceived*
> *Silly skunk with your tail raised—*
> *You're not a peacock!*

(SKRUYU)

Written by Skruyu at the age of fourteen, this haiku is the last he composed on natural subjects. It is said that the experience left him somewhat cynical.

> *Thanksgiving Day comes*
> *My kinfolk gather to feast*
> *We give them the bird!*

(SKRUYU)

So overwhelming is the poet's affection for his relatives that he is able, here, to suppress it only through the employment of a matter-of-fact, almost documentary, style as he portrays the joys of the holiday ritual.

A young girl bending
To wash herself in the lake
Behold the full moon!

(SNIKI)

Here we find Sniki addressing his favorite subjects—the water and the sky. His displeasure with the girl for marring this scene is obvious in every syllable.

The Polish night owl
Puts its beak under its wing
And falls from the limb.

(KLUTZI)

This verse, written by Klutzi in 1971, has since been banned in Japan. Klutzi went on permanent leave of absence from his status as a freshman in one of the regional schools of haiku a year after it appeared in print. His studies were not going well and he foresaw his premature departure from the school. Out of spite (one can only surmise) he cast a worthless Polish joke into haiku form and got it published in the local journal of verse. When the editors learned what had happened they were first chagrined and then unemployed. The haiku was banned. Klutzi fell into the habit of loitering in the barrooms of Sapporo, telling the story of his infamous "Polish haiku" to anyone willing to buy him a drink. Doomed to permanent and everlasting dishonor, he may well go down in history as the Archangel of Haiku.

The mountain people
Giving their thanks to the One
Who makes the moon shine.

(SPANKI)

The moon occupies a special place in Japanese culture. Early in life, schoolchildren learn to make a moon, and, as in our culture, the moon emblem is carved into the doors of important buildings.

> *His wife having left him*
> *I see my neighbor out back*
> *Whipping his dog.*

> (BLESSU)

This verse reveals the universality of true haiku. It was written by Blessu in 1684 and, despite the fact that this is a very active and "cluttered" verse, it is instantly understood by schoolboys in such unlikely areas as rural Alabama.

> *A farting duel*
> *My cousin missed me but did*
> *Blow out the candle.*

> (BLASTU)

This poem of Blastu's is rare in the world of haiku in that it recounts the equally rare involvement of a student of haiku in personal combat. Blastu never spoke of the duel again; thus we don't know who emerged as the winner (if, indeed, anyone could be considered a winner in such a situation).

Shots boom in the night
  Can it be that my neighbors
   Do not love music?

(BINKI)

It is doubtful that anyone had resorted to shooting because of Binki's habit of plucking the mandolin. The verse is cited to illustrate that although the poet's emotions are not supposed to assert themselves in his verses, they often do. The possibility that his neighbors *might* have felt hostility toward him upset the poet deeply, for Binki was one of the great pacifists of his time.

Farmer prays for rain
  Hot lightning flashes by him
   His water comes down.

(BLASTU)

The traditional Japanese caste system had five strata: noblemen, warriors, farmers, artisans, and merchants. While the other four groups offered a rich variety of prayers to Buddha, the farmers invariably pleaded for rain. Rice growers never seem to have enough water. It is conceivable, as the poet suggests in this verse, that the Great One would tire of this repetitous begging and zing one or two of them from time to time.

> *She's begun a hope chest*
> *Many fine things wait their turn*
> *To get in her box.*

(NITO)

This is a peculiar poem in that it is predicated on animism, or the idea that objects have a will of their own. This view, of course, is common in primitive cultures but the modern Japanese, like the American, rejects it. Yet, strangely enough, there are those in both countries who insist that objects such as those referred to in the verse *do* have a mind of their own.

> *Looming in the fog*
> *An outhouse comes into view*
> *Oh! Hi Beverly!*

(ONNŌ)

This verse aptly conveys the excitement of taking walks in the early morning when thick fog lies heavy on the landscape. As objects come into view, one cannot discern their identity with certainty. And, as one gets closer to them, their identities may change several times. In this case, the object, in fact, turned out to be Beverly (translated, of course, from the Japanese, "Beveri").

Onnō's "blind man" verse is an extension of this same theme. The poet was intrigued by things which appear not to be what they are:

> *The blind man walking*
> *By the fish market. He bows*
> *To ladies not there.*

Onnō had been observing the movements of a blind man proceeding slowly and methodically along the street. Trying to place himself in the blind man's situation, he wonders why the latter has made a mistake.

> *The itch that I had*
> *When I married has since gone*
> *But still I scratch it.*

> (SCRUFTI)

A truly universal haiku. It is every married man's discovery that the major difference in the quality of life between the bachelor and the wife-taker is that the latter has a perpetual supply of clean nether-garments. Beyond this, the verse says very little, though for some reason it seems to prompt a bittersweet twinge of regret among older readers.

> *On the birdcage floor,*
> *The verse that I wrote for her*
> *But can the bird read?*

> (KLUTZI)

The poet knows, of course, that no bird can read. He is pleased, however, that his naïve girl friend has somehow intuitively recognized the beauty of his poems and wishes to share them with her pet bird, much as a child would invite a cherished doll to "share" her lunch with her. One is

astounded, continually, by the insights of such
poets, and one senses that it is only the humility accompanying great wisdom which keeps
the obvious theme of male superiority from
surfacing.

> *She wants to show me*
> *The little man in the boat*
> *I wait by the lake.*

(OSOSO)

In the springtime of his life, Ososo fell in love
with and briefly courted Itchi Kuzzi, the
daughter of an itinerant fan painter from Masuda.
Unfortunately, their brief relationship was char-
acterized by misunderstandings. On this par-
ticular day, Ososo waited past sundown but there
was no boat, no little man, and, alas, no Kuzzi.

> *In the pecan grove,*
> *The bellowing of the bull—*
> *The nutting season.*

(BASSO)

The bull, who knows that the grove which
serves as his pasture will soon be invaded by the
pickers, is protesting. His bellowing also serves as
the clarion call announcing the invasion of Autumn's cold winds which will cut like a knife.

A lover's knee slips
And into the world there comes
Another clumsy clod.

(NITO)

In the postwar period of Japan, Nito was elevated to an office roughly equivalent to that of England's Poet Laureate. This occurred at the time the Japanese government mounted a sweeping campaign of birth control. This verse, which appeared in public places, on cigarette cards, and on the backs of men's toiletry containers, was designed to shame the male population into taking a more cautious approach in their relations with members of the female population. The program was immensely successful, owing, in no small part, to this haiku. It so happened, however, that Nito's brother-in-law, Sosumi, made a small fortune selling no-skid floor mats as a result of the verse's popularity. Though intent was never established on Nito's part, he was dismissed from his position but is today a very wealthy man.

With its talcum cap
The wart on her neck bears our
Hearts to Mount Fuji.

(BLESSU)

This haiku, written by Blessu in 1659, has been revived by Nipponese soldiers in all of Japan's modern wars. It is, of course, patriotic to a degree rarely seen in acceptable haiku. So compelling is the imagery, however, that critics most often overlook the inherent nationalism in the poem.

> *Am I familiar*
> *With those ice cubes with the holes?*
> *Crumb! I married one.*

> (KLUTZI)

This haiku has puzzled many readers. Is the poet actually saying that his wife is a cold little piece of ice? Hoshi did not think so, nor did Hito, or Wasu, or Kotomaki, or Benjo, or Bissa, or any of the lesser poets in the author's region.

Mirror on the wall
My fearless mother-in-law
Faces you squarely.

(BLESSU)

Here we see the poet noticing his wife's mother at her daily toilette, and he is moved by the realization that this is something she must do every day of her life. Blessu confided to his diary some years later that, until this moment (which prompted the verse), he had been unable to feel any respect for this woman who so often visited his home. This experience, however, impressed him deeply, as the poem clearly shows. In his diary, where his impressions were not refined and stylized to attain poetic form, he wrote simply:

"By the Great Buddha! You do have to admire the old ———° after all."

° Here, unfortunately, the poet interjected an idiom, or localism, perhaps, which defied our translators. No matter; it was, as one may correctly infer from its context, a high compliment.

SOCIAL CHANGE AND
THE MODERN POETS

Though the bulk and tradition of haiku poetry addresses itself to simple, natural subjects, there is no subject matter forbidden to the haiku poet. In this final section are presented a few selections of the modern poets based on a variety of new topics.

> *A basketball game*
> *On the hardwood floor grown men*
> *Dribbling in their shorts.*

(SHORTĪ)

Professor Blyth (1964) presented Seishi's verse on Rugby, proclaiming it one of the very few in existence on the subject of sports. Since that door has been opened, we offer the first on *this* sport. It was written by Shortī, who tried very hard to make the team while attending Kobi PS in 1959.

Stay away from the
Xerox, Marge; one of you
Is quite sufficient.

(TUSHI)

This verse by Tushi was one of many written while he was engaged in a business training program under American auspices in Tokyo. He also wrote the following:

Hungry silverfish
Found our Quarterly Report
Quite interesting.

They gave my uncle
A retirement watch which
Didn't work either.

One of the most beloved of modern haiku is the following poem by Nuki, the great-grandson of the old master Nito:

Love by TV light
I hope that we will be done
Before Sermonette.

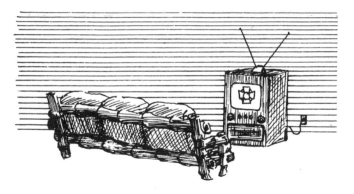

Reaffirming basic religious and moral values, as this verse so effectively does, it is said to have put an entire generation of concerned parents at ease. Not only does the young poet here verbalize his own sense of the importance of traditional values, but we are assured that his companion is also encouraging him to hurry. Verily, Nuki is the Pat Boone of his country.

But without doubt, the verses of the rural poets as they experience the effects of Japanese industrialization and technological advancement have been the most poignant. Consider this verse by Cashu:

> *Taking her picture*
> *The Polaroid makes a groan*
> *And then it spits up.*

Or this one by Moralesi:

> *The new physician*
> *Wants a bottle of urine*
> *The last one took cash.*

And, finally, we present a modern verse better than most currently written, in that it conveys the sadness of the Zen outlook which must always be inherent in the best verses:

> *There goes my neighbor,*
> *Arms filled with groceries and*
> *No beer in his house.*

(BUZO)

How it must have saddened the old poet, to see such close evidence of the confusion of basic values brought to his village by the zealous new breed of social workers. Indeed, we all must ask what can come of a world in which foodstuffs take precedence over the values of the "Old Way."